ARACHNID WORLD
SCORPIONS
SANDRA MARKLE

ARMORED STINGERS

LERNER PUBLICATIONS COMPANY MINNEAPOLIS

FOR CURIOUS KIDS EVERYWHERE

ACKNOWLEDGMENTS

The author would like to thank Dr. Doug Gaffin and Dr. Marielle Hoefnagels, University of Oklahoma; Mark Newton, Australia Scorpion Forum; and Dr. Simon Pollard, Canterbury Museum, Christchurch, New Zealand, for sharing their expertise and enthusiasm. A special thanks to Skip Jeffery for his support during the creation of this book.

Lerner Publications Company
A division of Lerner Publishing Group, Inc.
241 First Avenue North
Minneapolis, MN 55401 U.S.A.

Website address: www.lernerbooks.com

Library of Congress Cataloging-in-Publication Data

Markle, Sandra.
    Scorpions : armored stingers/ by Sandra Markle.
      p.   cm. — (Arachnid world)
    Includes bibliographical references and index.
    ISBN 978–0–7613–5037–8 (lib. bdg. : alk. paper)
    1. Scorpions—Juvenile literature. I. Title.
  QL458.7.M35 2011
  595.4'6—dc22   2010004275

Manufactured in the United States of America
1 - DP - 12/31/10

# CONTENTS

AN ARACHNID'S WORLD

WELCOME TO THE WORLD OF ARACHNIDS

(ah-RACK-nidz). They can be found everywhere on Earth except Antarctica.

So how can you tell if an animal is an arachnid rather than a relative like the crustacean? Both arachnids and crustaceans belong to a group of animals called arthropods (AR-throh-podz). All the animals in this group share some traits. They have bodies divided into segments, have jointed legs, and have a stiff exoskeleton. This is a skeleton on the outside like a suit of armor. But one way to tell if an animal is an arachnid is to count its legs and main body parts. While not every adult arachnid has eight legs, most do. Arachnids also have two main body parts. Adult crustaceans, like the reef lobster *(right)*, also have eight legs, but they have three main body parts.

This book is about arachnids called scorpions. Like the emperor scorpion *(facing page)*, all scorpions are venomous. They can inject a liquid poison through a stinger on their tail end. Scorpions use venom to kill prey and defend themselves.

SCORPION FACT

A scorpion's body temperature rises and falls with the temperature around it. It must warm up to be active.

OUTSIDE AND INSIDE

ON THE OUTSIDE

Take a close look at the outside of an adult female marbled scorpion. Scorpions have just two main body parts: the cephalothorax (sef-uh-loh-THOR-ax) and the abdomen. The exoskeleton covers a scorpion's whole body. It is made up of many hard plates connected by stretchy tissue. This lets the scorpion bend and move. Check out the key parts that most scorpions share.

CEPHALOTHORAX

PEDIPALPS:
These are
a pair of pincers.
They are the largest
parts extending from
the scorpion's
body.

EYES:
These detect
light and send
signals to the brain for
sight. Scorpions have
two large eyes in the
middle of their
heads.

CHELICERAE
(keh-LISS-ee-ray):
These are a pair of
small clawlike parts near the
mouth. They have teeth along
the inner edges. Chelicerae are
used to grab and crush a prey's
harder parts. They are
also used to pull
off small bits
of food.

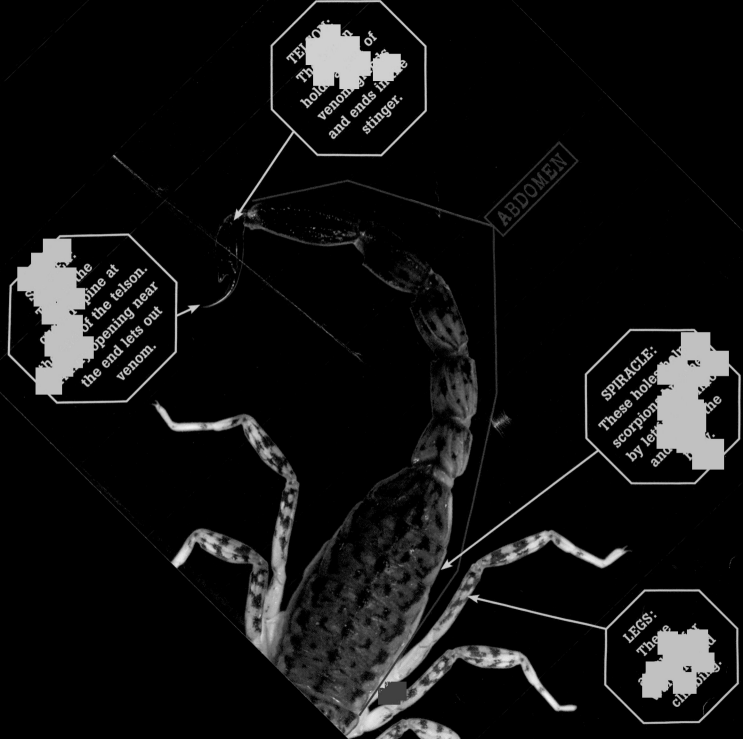

ON THE INSIDE

Look at this drawing of the inside
of an adult female scorpion.

HEART:
This muscular tube
pumps blood toward the
head and the abdomen
and the book lungs. Blood
flows throughout the
body and back to
the heart.

**HEPATOPANCREAS
(heh-pat-oh-PAN-
kree-us):**
This organ produces the
digestive juices. It is
also a storage site for
digested food.

BRAIN:
The brain
receives messages
from body parts and
sends signals back
to them.

**PHARYNX
(FAR-inks):**
This muscular
tube pumps food
into the body's
digestive
system.

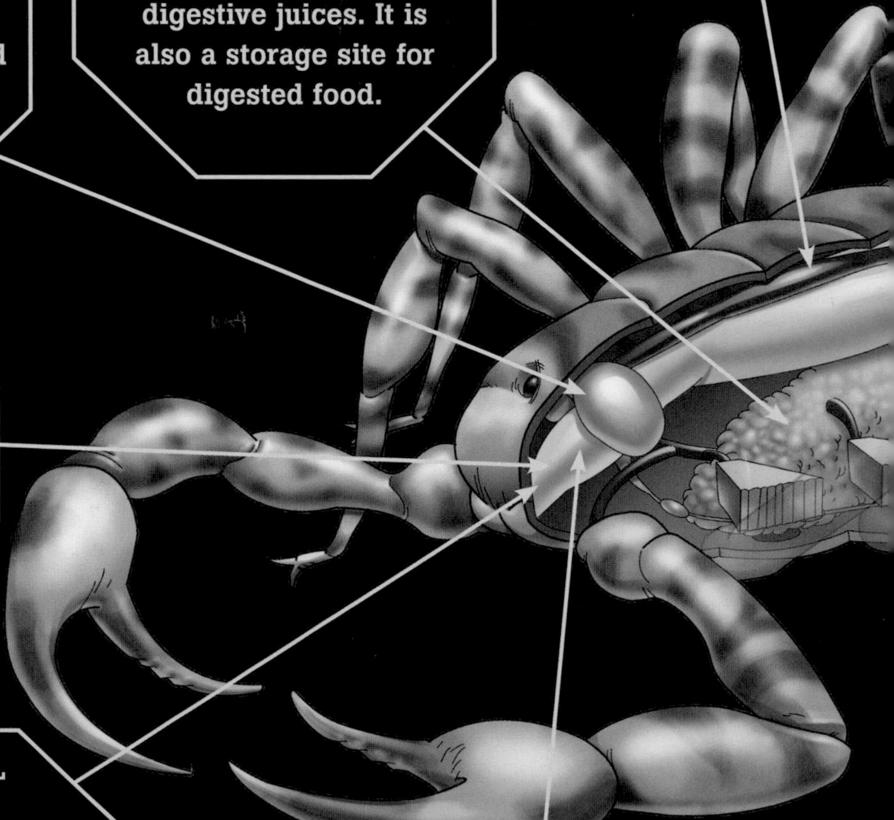

**PREORAL
CAVITY:**
This is space
where digestive juices
start to break down
food. Special hairs
block hard bits.

ESOPHAGUS:
Food passes
through this tube on
the way to the stomach.

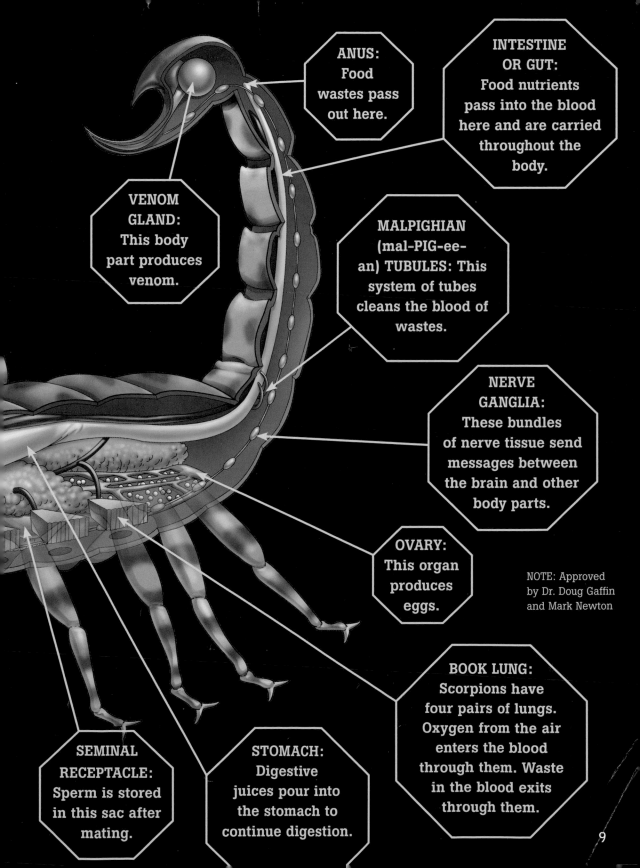

ANUS:
Food
wastes pass
out here.

INTESTINE
OR GUT:
Food nutrients
pass into the blood
here and are carried
throughout the
body.

VENOM
GLAND:
This body
part produces
venom.

MALPIGHIAN
(mal-PIG-ee-
an) TUBULES: This
system of tubes
cleans the blood of
wastes.

NERVE
GANGLIA:
These bundles
of nerve tissue send
messages between
the brain and other
body parts.

OVARY:
This organ
produces
eggs.

NOTE: Approved
by Dr. Doug Gaffin
and Mark Newton

BOOK LUNG:
Scorpions have
four pairs of lungs.
Oxygen from the air
enters the blood
through them. Waste
in the blood exits
through them.

SEMINAL
RECEPTACLE:
Sperm is stored
in this sac after
mating.

STOMACH:
Digestive
juices pour into
the stomach to
continue digestion.

A scorpion's exoskeleton has a waxy substance that makes it waterproof. The exoskeleton also has special chemicals that do something else. They make the scorpions glow.

Compare this bark scorpion when it's in sunlight *(top)* and when it's exposed to ultraviolet (UV) light *(bottom)*. Except for newborns, all scorpions glow blue green or yellow green in UV light.

Special chemicals in their exoskeletons cause them to glow. Scorpions are active at night when most of the light is UV starlight. Glowing in UV light might help mates find one another.

SCORPION FACT

About two thousand different kinds of scorpions exist.

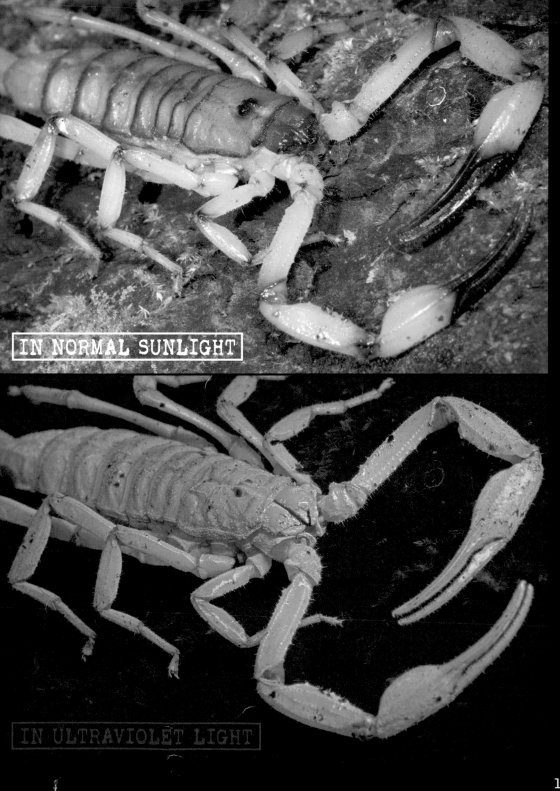

IN NORMAL SUNLIGHT

IN ULTRAVIOLET LIGHT

BECOMING ADULTS

Like all arachnids, baby scorpions become adults through incomplete metamorphosis (me–teh–MOR–feh–sus). *Metamorphosis* means "change." A scorpion's life includes three stages: egg; immature, or scorpling; and adult. Unlike many other kinds of arachnids, females keep their eggs inside their bodies while the young develop.

> **SOME ARTHROPODS GO THROUGH COMPLETE METAMORPHOSIS.** The stages are egg, larva, pupa, and adult. Each stage looks and behaves very differently.

Some kinds of scorpions, like the common yellow scorpion, produce eggs with lots of yolk. The young get all the food energy they need from the yolk. Others, like the bark scorpion, produce eggs with a smaller amount of yolk. Part of their supply of food comes from their mother's body and passes to the young through the egg lining. Still other kinds of scorpions, like the Flinders Ranges scorpion *(right)*, produce eggs with little or no yolk. Then the mother's ovary develops nipplelike parts. Each baby scorpion grips one of these with its chelicerae. Food is pumped from the mother's body into its own body.

Once the young are fully developed, the female gives birth to her litter of young. The newborns emerge, one at a time, through her gonopore (female reproductive opening).

FLINDERS RANGES SCORPION

NEWBORN SCORPLINGS

How long a baby scorpion develops before birth depends on the kind of scorpion it is. Cuban striped scorpions develop for less than two months. Yellow-legged creeping scorpions develop for about eighteen months.

Newborn scorplings, like these Flinders Ranges scorpion young, are tiny, paler versions of their parents. At this stage, they have no venom. So after they're born, they quickly climb up their mother's legs and ride on her back. She is armed, so being with her keeps them safe.

SCORPION FACT

The number of young in a litter varies with the kind of scorpion. The average is about twenty-five babies per female.

Scorplings stay on their mother's back until after their first molt. That's when they shed their soft newborn covering. After that, they are able to produce venom and to sting.

After a scorpling goes off on its own, it catches prey and grows bigger. In time, it grows so big its exoskeleton becomes tight. Then, like this scorpling *(right)*, it molts again. Its exoskeleton splits open, and the scorpling crawls out. A new protective coat already covers its body. Its new exoskeleton is soft at first. So the scorpling's heart beats harder, forcing blood into different parts of its body to stretch the soft exoskeleton. Its new coat hardens over its body, which has expanded to be a little bigger than it really is. This way, the scorpling has room to grow before it needs to molt again. After its final molt, a scorpling becomes an adult. Only adults are able to mate and produce young.

SCORPION FACT

Scorplings that lose a leg shortly after a molt may develop a new part of that leg. But they don't regrow an entire leg. Other immature arachnids, like spiderlings, that lose a leg may regrow a complete new leg.

SCORPION FACT

The number of
molts needed to
reach adulthood varies with
different kinds of scorpions.
Most scorpions become
adults after five or
six molts.

OLD EXOSKELETON

SCORPLING

ARMED AND READY

The focus of a scorpion's life is staying safe and catching prey. Most scorpions are colored to blend in with their environment. This lets them hide from bigger predators and ambush prey. That's how this giant hairy scorpion was able to stay safe and catch a gecko.

While a scorpion is in hiding, it keeps track of what is going on around it. Scientists believe that its big eyes only see shadowy shapes. But the scorpion has lots of sensitive hairs on its body. These help it sense vibrations (small movements) passing through the ground or the air. The vibrations alert it to something moving nearby. The stronger the vibrations are, the bigger the animal. The bigger animal may even be a predator. Weaker vibrations mean that what's moving is small enough to be prey.

SENSITIVE HAIR
(ENLARGED)

SCORPION FACT

Some kinds of scorpions dig underground to hide from predators. Temperatures are cooler underground. Scorpions in hot deserts go underground to escape the daytime heat.

Either way, the scorpion is armed to attack. It has pincerlike pedipalps to tear and crush. Some, like this rock scorpion, have giant pedipalps.

PEDIPALPS

A scorpion's greatest weapon is its stinger, which injects venom. The venom comes out a tiny hole near the stinger's tip. The venom paralyzes or kills prey—even prey bigger than the scorpion. Venom can also help the scorpion escape predators. This lesser brown scorpion's sting probably won't kill or even paralyze the meerkat. But the pain the sting causes is likely to make the meerkat let go of it. Then the scorpion can escape.

STINGER

ON THE HUNT

It's fall in Texas. The female striped bark scorpion *(right)* has only recently become an adult. She's as big as she's going to grow—about 3 inches (7 centimeters) long—and has a big appetite. Worms, spiders, crickets, other small insects, and smaller arachnids are all fair game. Still, she doesn't hunt during the hot daytime. While it's hot, she hides in a crevice in a fallen log. Then when the day's shadows lengthen and the air cools, she crawls out. As she walks, the sensors on her feet detect vibrations. They tell her when an insect is moving nearby. She stops, stays still, and waits.

SCORPION FACT

The most venomous kinds of scorpions are found in Africa and the Middle East. The Arizona bark scorpion is the most venomous kind of scorpion in the United States. Even so, in a human, its venom usually only causes numbness and tingling near the sting site.

She waits until a grasshopper comes close. ZING! She flicks her tail to deliver a dose of venom to her prey. This kills the grasshopper.

She uses her chelicerae to crush and tear off part of the insect. She moves the food into the preoral cavity. Digestive juices pour in to liquefy the food. Hairs in the preoral cavity filter out any hard waste bits. These may be parts of the grasshopper's exoskeleton. The waste bits are pressed together and removed by the chelicerae. The pharynx pumps the liquid food through the tiny mouth opening *(below)* and into the esophagus. From there the food moves on through the digestive system. More digestive juices completely break down the food. The parts of food that supply energy to the scorpion pass into the blood and spread to all body parts. Scorpions also get most of the water they need from their food. Food wastes pass out the anus.

SCORPION FACT

Scorpions use up food energy very slowly. They can go a month or longer between meals.

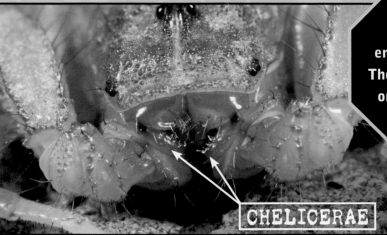

CHELICERAE

FIGHT AND FLEE

As the day gets brighter and hotter, the female striped bark scorpion seeks a shady hiding place. She doesn't notice the lizard because it is sitting perfectly still. Finally, the lizard moves, and she senses it. But it's too late for her to run away. The lizard grabs the scorpion's head end. In a flash, the female flicks her tail and injects venom into the lizard. The lizard drops her.

The fall doesn't hurt her. She scurries away fast, squeezes under a rock, and escapes.

SCORPION FACT

A scorpion's tough exoskeleton acts like armor plating to protect its internal body parts.

A FAMILY MATTER

All through the hot day, the adult female striped bark scorpion stays hidden. Then, as the air cools, she goes hunting again. Wherever she goes, she gives off special chemicals, called pheromones (FAIR-eh-mohnz). These tell males she's a female striped bark scorpion and ready to mate. One night, as if sensing perfume, an adult male striped bark scorpion picks up her signal. When he gets close to her, he shudders. This creates a special air movement that the female's sensitive hairs detect. The female accepts him by staying still. The courtship begins.

As though dancing, the male grabs the female's pedipalps. The female backs up. The male pulls her forward. They circle. The male also uses his chelicerae to rub the female's chelicerae. All the while, the male's pectines (special comblike sensors) tap the ground, searching for a smooth, flat surface. When he finds one, he deposits a mass of sticky sperm (male reproductive cells). The mass sticks to the flat surface. The male guides the female over the sperm, which enter her body through her gonopore.

For many kinds of scorpions, the courtship may last for hours.

MALE

FEMALE

Female striped bark scorpions may produce as many as fifty eggs at a time. She received more of the male's sperm than that, though. She will store the rest of the sperm in her seminal receptacle until she's given birth and is ready to get pregnant again.

As soon as the male's sperm combines with the female's eggs, the baby scorpions start to develop inside their eggs. The eggs stay inside the female's body. The babies receive part of the food they need from their egg's yolk. They receive water and more food from the female's body. Even while she's pregnant, the female needs to keep hunting prey like this cockroach.

SCORPION FACT

Males may mate several times during their lifetime. A female scorpion may mate just once and produce four or five litters.

Winter arrives with cold days and even colder nights. The female striped bark scorpion spends a lot of time hiding in cracks or under leaf litter. She still hunts, though, whenever the weather warms up enough for her to be active.

Inside her, the baby scorpions grow slowly. She needs nearly eight months for them to fully develop. By spring the weather is warming up. Her babies are ready to be born. The prey insects that hid away during the winter are becoming active. Their young are hatching too. So plenty of food will be available for the young scorpions.

How long baby scorpions take to develop varies. Some kinds take just a couple of months. Others need more than a year to develop.

A HIDING ARIZONA STRIPETAIL SCORPION

SCORPION BABIES

As the birth begins, the female lifts her cephalothorax. Then she arches the front half of her abdomen. She puts her first two pairs of legs, like cupped hands, under her gonopore. One by one, her young push through this opening. A baby scorpion has a soft exoskeleton, so the female catches each one with her legs. This keeps them from hitting the hard ground and getting hurt. Then the youngsters climb up their mother's legs onto her back. They can't produce venom yet. And their pedipalps can't pinch. Their mother doesn't take care of them, but just being with her keeps them safe.

SCORPION FACT

Newborn scorpions lack a water-resistant coat. They could quickly dry out and die. The babies soak up moisture that their mother gives off through her exoskeleton.

For about two weeks after their birth, the babies stay on their mother's back. They don't eat. They get the energy they need to grow a bit bigger from food nutrients stored inside their bodies. If any babies fall off, they hurry to climb back onto their mother again. At this stage, they would be very easy prey for any predator.

Finally, the babies molt, shedding their first soft body covering. Underneath they have a hard, water-resistant exoskeleton. Their pedipalps can pinch. And their bodies produce venom. The scorplings may leave within a day or two. Or they may stay on their mother's back a little longer. Once they do leave, they scurry away as fast as they can. This scorpling *(right)* is hiding under a leaf. It waits to ambush even tinier prey. And it stays hidden out of sight of predators.

SCORPION FACT

After they've molted, they are no longer protected by their mother. She might even eat any scorplings she can catch.

Predators live wherever in the world scorplings grow up. Centipedes, mice, and snakes are on the prowl for them. Scorplings, like this immature salt lake scorpion, meet threats head on. After all, they're armed and wearing a suit of armor.

The scorplings that survive and catch prey grow bigger. They continue to grow and molt every few months for a year or more. Finally, they molt one last time and become adults. They mate, and the female carries her young with her—before and after birth. Finally, the scorplings, armed for catching prey and for defense, set off. They continue the scorpion's cycle of life.

SCORPIONS AND OTHER ARMED ARACHNIDS

SCORPIONS BELONG TO A GROUP, or order, of arachnids called Scorpiones. All the nearly two thousand kinds of scorpions are venomous. Each is deadly to its prey—usually insects. Only a very few kinds of scorpions produce a venom that causes a serious reaction in people. Usually that venom is only dangerous for children or adults with other health problems.

SCIENTISTS GROUP living and extinct animals with others that are similar. So scorpions are classified this way:

kingdom: Animalia
phylum: Arthropoda
class: Arachnida
order: Scorpiones
family: Scorpionidae

HELPFUL OR HARMFUL? Scorpions are both. They're helpful because they eat a lot of insects. They help control the numbers of insect pests. Scorpions may be even more helpful in the future. Researchers are extracting chemicals from scorpion venom. They're studying how these chemicals can be used in the treatment of some types of cancer. Scorpions with the strongest venom, like the yellow fat-tailed scorpion, are found in Africa. Like all scorpions, they only sting in self-defense, but their venom is strong enough to make people ill. Rarely, the venom even kills.

HOW BIG IS a striped bark scorpion? A female is about 3 inches (7.5 cm) long.

MORE ARMED DEFENDERS

Compare a scorpion's defenses to the way these other arachnids defend themselves.

Australian funnel web spiders are among the world's most venomous 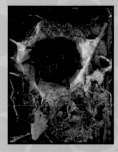 spiders. These medium to large spiders of Australia and the South Pacific islands deliver their venom with a bite rather than a sting. But producing venom uses up food energy. So to avoid having to bite in self-defense, they build a silk-lined burrow and place traps of sticky silk at the entrance. They hide inside their burrow and only rush out to kill prey caught in their lines. Then they scurry back inside to safety.

Giant vinegaroons have long tails but lack a stinger. Instead, they  spray a mist of vinegar-like acid from a gland at the base of their tail. This acid isn't likely to kill a predator, such as a bird, but it is irritating. That's usually enough to make the predator pull back. Then the giant vinegaroon can slip under a rock or into a tight crevice to escape. These natives of the southwestern United States only spray as a last resort. They mainly stay safe by hunting their insect prey at night. Their dark color lets them hide in plain sight.

Goliath birdeater tarantulas are the world's largest spiders. These  hairy natives of South American rain forests have two ways to defend themselves. Some of their hairs are barbed (spiky). When the tarantulas are threatened, they turn their backs on their enemies. Then they kick their bodies with their back legs to flick off these barbed hairs. The hairs are irritating and can blind a predator if they strike its eyes. If the predator still attacks, the tarantula uses its ultimate weapon—its venomous bite.

GLOSSARY

abdomen: the back end of an arachnid where systems for digestion and reproduction are located

adult: the final stage of an arachnid's life cycle. Arachnids are able to reproduce at this stage.

anus: an opening to get rid of wastes

book lungs: thin, flat folds of tissue where blood circulates. When air passes through them, oxygen enters the scorpion's blood. Waste also exits through these lungs. Scorpions have four pairs of book lungs.

brain: the organ that receives messages from sense organs and other body parts and sends signals to control them

cephalothorax: the front end of an arachnid where the mouth, the brain, and the eyes are located. Legs are also attached to the cephalothorax.

chelicerae: a pair of small clawlike parts near the mouth. They are sharp-tipped and have teeth on the inner edge. They are used to grab and crush prey and to pull off small bits of food.

egg: a female reproductive cell; also the name given to the first stage of an arachnid's life cycle

esophagus: a tube through which food passes on the way to the stomach

exoskeleton: the protective, armorlike skeleton covering the outside of an arachnid's body

eyes: sensory organs that detect light and send signals to the brain for sight

gonopore: the female reproductive opening

heart: the muscular tube that pumps blood throughout the body

hepatopancreas: a body part that produces digestive juices and is a storage site for digested food

incomplete metamorphosis: a process of development in which the young look and behave much like a small adult except that they are unable to reproduce. Stages include egg; immature, or scorpling; and adult.

intestine: a tube through which food passes into the blood to be carried throughout the body

legs: limbs used for walking and climbing. The joints near the feet have sensors that detect vibrations.

malpighian tubules: a system of tubes that cleans the blood of wastes and dumps them into the intestine

molt: the process of shedding the exoskeleton

ovary: the body part that produces eggs

pectines: a pair of comblike sensors

pedipalps: pincers that extend from the scorpion's body. They are used to catch and crush prey. They are also used during courtship and for defense.

pharynx: a muscular body part that expands and contracts to create a pump to pull food into the body's digestive system

pheromones: chemical scents given off as a form of communication

predator: an animal that is a hunter

preoral cavity: the space where digestive juices start to break down food. Special hairs block hard bits from going through the mouth.

prey: an animal that a predator catches to eat

scorpling: an immature scorpion

seminal receptacle: the place in a female's body where sperm is stored after mating

sperm: a male reproductive cell

stinger: the curved spine at the end of the telson. A tiny opening near the end lets out venom.

stomach: an organ where digestive juices break down food

telson: the last segment of the tail that holds the anus, the stinger, and the venom glands

venom glands: body parts that produce venom

vibrations: small movements in the air or in the ground

DIGGING DEEPER

To keep on investigating scorpions, explore these books and online sites.

BOOKS

Halfmann, Janet. *Nature's Predators: Scorpions*. Farmington Hills, MI: KidHaven Press, 2002. Take another look at scorpions in their role as predators.

Hillyard, P. D. *Spiders and Scorpions*. Clifton, NJ: Reader's Digest Young Families, 1995. Compare scorpions to spiders with special 3-D peeks inside these arachnids.

Lassieur, Allison. *Scorpions: The Sneaky Stinger*. Danbury, CT: Franklin Watts, 2000. Survey types of scorpions living in different parts of the world. Also, go along with a researcher on a scorpion hunt.

Singer, Marilyn. *Venom*. Minneapolis: Millbrook Press, 2007. Scorpions are included in this book with other animals that sting and bite.

Souza, D. M. *Packed with Poison*. Minneapolis: Millbrook Press, 2006. This is a brief look at venomous animals large and small.

MORE FROM SANDRA MARKLE

INSECT WORLD:
Diving Beetles
Hornets
Locusts
Luna Moths
Mosquitoes
Praying Mantises
Stick Insects
Termites

WEBSITES

Desert USA: Scorpions

http://www.desertusa.com/oct96/du_scorpion.html

This site is packed with information about scorpions living in desert areas of the United States.

Emperor Scorpion

http://www.arkive.org/emperor-scorpion/pandinus-imperator description.html

Click on the video links to observe moments in the lives of emperor scorpions. Don't miss babies being born.

Kids Health

http://kidshealth.org/kid/ill_injure/bugs/scorpion.html

Read all sorts of scorpion facts and learn what to do if a scorpion stings you.

LERNER 𝒆 SOURCE™

Visit www.lernersource.com for free, downloadable arachnid diagrams, research assignments to use with this series, and additional information about arachnid scientific names.

National Geographic

http://www .nationalgeographic.com/coloringbook/scorpions.html

Download and print this coloring page of a scorpion in the act catching its prey.

Scorpion Enchanted Learning

http://www.enchantedlearning.com/cgi-bin/paint/kS/subjects/arachnids/scorpion/Scorpionprintout.shtml

Discover interesting facts about scorpions. Use the interactive chart to color a picture of a scorpion's body parts.

SCORPION ACTIVITY

WHO'S THERE?

All scorpions, like this Brazilian scorpion *(right)*, are covered with sensitive hairs to detect vibrations through the ground and air. Although nowhere near as sensitive, the touch and pressure sensors in your skin let you feel when something moves near you. This activity will let you explore how the scorpion judges where to grab prey. You'll also discover how the scorpion tells whether something is small enough to tackle safely or if the prey is so big that the scorpion might need to defend itself.

1. Work with a partner.

2. Fold a sheet of notebook paper in half, or use a piece of cardboard.

3. Sit in a chair, and close your eyes.

4. Have your partner stand about an arm's length away. Then have your partner fan your face first on one side and then on the other. Try to point in the direction of the airflow.

5. Next, have your partner fan your face gently and then briskly. Try to judge when the airflow is strongest.

6. Discuss what you discovered with your partner.

SENSITIVE HAIRS

INDEX

PHOTO ACKNOWLEDGMENTS

The images in this book are used with the permission of: © Franco Banfi/SeaPics.com, p. 4; © Daniel Heuclin/NHPA/Photoshot, pp. 5, 26–27, 41 (middle and bottom); © Mark A. Newton, pp. 6–7, 12–13, 15, 17, 38, 39; © Bill Hauser/Independent Picture Service, pp. 8–9; © Piotr Naskrecki/Minden Pictures, pp. 11 (both), 47; © Albert Lleal/Minden Pictures, p. 18; © Paul Zahl/ National Geographic Stock, pp. 18–19; © Stephen Dalton/NHPA/Photoshot, p. 20; © Dennis Kunkel Microscopy, Inc./Visuals Unlimited, Inc., p. 21 (top); © Solvin Zankl/naturepl.com, p. 21 (bottom); © Francesco Tomasinelli/Photo Researchers, Inc., p. 23; © Steve Graser/Visuals Unlimited, Inc., p. 24; © Michael Francis Photography/Animals Animals, p. 25; © Dr. Kojun Kanda, pp. 28–29; © Charles Melton/Visuals Unlimited, Inc., pp. 30–31; © Joe McDonald/Visuals Unlimited, Inc., pp. 32–33; © Dante Fenolio/Photo Researchers, Inc., pp. 34–35; © Francesco Tomasinelli/Natural Visions, pp. 36–37; © Patti Murray/Animals Animals, p. 41 (top).

Front cover: © Rick & Nora Bowers/Visuals Unlimited, Inc.